THE DEEP BLUE OF NEPTUNE

Wick Poetry First Book Series

DAVID HASSLER, EDITOR

The Deep Blue of Neptune by Terry Belew — Alison Hawthorne Deming, Judge
Opium and Ambergris by Colin Dekeersgieter — Marilyn Chin, Judge
Fraternal Light: On Painting While Black by Arlene Keizer — Cornelius Eady, Judge
Sister Tongue زبان خواهر by Farnaz Fatemi — Tracy K. Smith, Judge
How Blood Works by Ellene Glenn Moore — Richard Blanco, Judge
On This Side of the Desert by Alfredo Aguilar — Natalie Diaz, Judge
The Many Names for Mother by Julia Kolchinsky Dasbach — Ellen Bass, Judge
Fugue Figure by Michael McKee Green — Khaled Mattawa, Judge
Even Years by Christine Gosnay — Angie Estes, Judge
hover over her by Leah Poole Osowski — Adrian Matejka, Judge
Translation by Matthew Minicucci — Jane Hirshfield, Judge
The Spectral Wilderness by Oliver Bendorf — Mark Doty, Judge
The Dead Eat Everything by Michael Mlekoday — Dorianne Laux, Judge
Wet by Carolyn Creedon — Edward Hirsch, Judge
The Local World by Mira Rosenthal — Maggie Anderson, Judge

MAGGIE ANDERSON, EDITOR EMERITA

Visible Heavens by Joanna Solfrian — Naomi Shihab Nye, Judge
The Infirmary by Edward Micus — Stephen Dunn, Judge
Far from Algiers by Djelloul Marbrook — Toi Derricotte, Judge
Constituents of Matter by Anna Leahy — Alberto Rios, Judge
Intaglio by Ariana-Sophia M. Kartsonis — Eleanor Wilner, Judge
Trying to Speak by Anele Rubin — Philip Levine, Judge
Rooms and Fields: Dramatic Monologues from the War in Bosnia by Lee Peterson — Jean Valentine, Judge
The Drowned Girl by Eve Alexandra — C. K. Williams, Judge
Back Through Interruption by Kate Northrop — Lynn Emanuel, Judge
Paper Cathedrals by Morri Creech — Li-Young Lee, Judge
The Gospel of Barbecue by Honorée Fanonne Jeffers — Lucille Clifton, Judge
Beyond the Velvet Curtain by Karen Kovacik — Henry Taylor, Judge
The Apprentice of Fever by Richard Tayson — Marilyn Hacker, Judge

The Deep Blue of Neptune

Poems by

Terry Belew

The Kent State University Press

Kent, Ohio

© 2025 by Terry Belew
All rights reserved
ISBN 978-1-60635-498-8
Manufactured in the United States of America

No part of this book may be used or reproduced, in any manner whatsoever, without written permission from the Publisher, except in the case of short quotations in critical reviews or articles.

The Wick Poetry Series is sponsored by the Stan and Tom Wick Poetry Center and the Department of English at Kent State University.

Cataloging information for this title is available at the Library of Congress.

29 28 27 26 25   5 4 3 2 1

CONTENTS

Foreword by Alison Hawthorne Deming   vii
October Preserves   1
Animal Science   3
In the Woods   5
The Anatomy of Envy   6
Considering Entropy   8
In the Atrium of the Children's Hospital   9
Modern Medicine   10
Architecture   11
Ask the Wind to Blow   12
The Fog of It   13
For Certain   14
Wish List While Reading the News on My Phone   16
Half-Staff   17
Departing in a Space Shuttle   18
Exhibit A   20
Legacy Waste   21
Tattoo Removal   23
Crowdsourcing   24
Doctor, Doctor   25
Child Drawings   26
Stars and Satellites   27
Perfidy   29
Cutting Wood   31
Wish List for a Deity   32
Whiskey Gospel   33
The Great Raccoon War   34
Drogue   35
The Anatomy of the Cold   36
Trash Pile   38
Bull Riders   39
Grim Sanity   40
Gunshot at the Neighbors'   41
The Deep Blue of Neptune   42

Detours 44
Broken Pantoum upon Getting a New Phone Number 45
Shudder 47
Dead Sweetheart 49
Wish List While Listening to Love Songs 50
While Driving 51
Night Song 52
Cigarette Vending Machine 54
Entropy's Ultimatum 55
Pest Control 57
Exhibit B 59
Wish List After Using a 3-D Printer 60
Traffic 61
The Anatomy of Forgiveness 63
Acknowledgments 65

FOREWORD
Alison Hawthorne Deming

A Seamus Heaney quotation has been making the rounds, and it strikes me as resonant with the poetry of Terry Belew: "We are made to live in at least two places at one time. . . . We should keep our feet on the ground to signify that nothing is beneath us, but also lift our eyes up to say nothing is beyond us."

Belew's poetry is grounded in the life of place, akin to Elizabeth Bishop in Nova Scotia, Frank O'Hara in Manhattan, or Wendell Berry in rural Kentucky. Belew, a longtime resident of small-town rural Missouri, brings his home place into the company of poets who have found in the grounding of place a window onto what lies beyond. His poems may begin in a narrative situation—"Some type of squash or melon / is growing from a mound / of chicken shit in the backyard"—then follow a chain of associations to a young woman's fentanyl-inflected vulnerability and a brutal threat. This portrait of place is no pastoral idyll, for in American life brutality lies just around the corner. How to keep empathy alive in such a world, how to be useful in such times, these are questions that drive Belew's poems.

>   . . . I know
> of no other animal that keeps poisoning
>
> itself, Sodium Nitrate and Yellow #5,
>   cheeseburgers and bourbon, the constant
> stream of shootings in the news
>
>   reminding me I'm alive. I know
> my genes scream for continuity
>   because my only purpose
> is to leave something useful.

The poems in *The Deep Blue of Neptune* connect empathically with the American heartland, the damage and peril of these times. He gets our cultural moment, our shared complicity in ruin. He has a gift for finding the occasion for a poem in the everyday. A trip to Walmart, a father fishing with his son, overhearing neighbors "fight then fuck," cleanup after an unspeakable car wreck, hunting for "stupid videos" may all serve as grounding for a poem. But the meditative journeys the poems make are breathtaking. They seem to me essayistic in the way they travel from narrative situation to the inwardness of a man working to be honest with himself. Life is hard to figure out, and, as in the poetry of Carl Phillips, Belew speaks lyrically of the wounds and uncertainty that make us human. And how in need of empathy.

Belew's formal artistry ranges to lyric poems, sonnets, a broken pantoum, three remarkable sestinas, and the invented forms of "Wish List After Using a 3-D Printer" and "Wish List for a Deity," among others. His "Exhibit A" and "Exhibit B" capture the velocity and anxiety of digital life. The voice may be self-effacing, yet it is playfully so, as if the poet were astonished to find gravity and levity dancing together at the local bar. Throughout the collection, language rings with crystalline clarity, spiked with striking metaphors: "our feet out of time like a solar clock / in a century of dark."

Nature, though damaged, continues to serve as template for constancy. Its inspiration lies as much in its "preening dormancy" as in its blooming. This rural community is a place where a woman "waters every quick-drying / flower in the children's graveyard," a place where no flowers bloom at the nearby landfill, a place where "the sun's chandelier crashes low," a place where katydids rouse envy for being so clear about how to live their lives. Nature is both wound and salve. Consider his exquisite sestina "Anatomy for Forgiveness" in which the act of buying bees for a backyard hive serves as balm for "being born to consume." Tenderness comes with the practice of giving back to nature:

> . . . I want to keep alive
> something small, something which had been born
> with a purpose other than to consume so
> I can atone for my existence.

The Deep Blue of Neptune is a powerful and moving debut collection, a book that is clear-eyed, unsentimental, and tender in the face of the brutalities of our time. For Terry Belew, the local is the lens through which the universal struggles of our mortal condition can be seen. And to see, really see, and find the artful words for that seeing is indeed to be of use.

OCTOBER PRESERVES

It is no thrill to listen
to an insolent child
play a kazoo. To clarify,
the raucous flinch
of sliding sounds slices
my temperament into smoke.
Not to disparage
elementary school music class,
but there's no defense
for that noise, no slake
in the hum of a few pennies'
worth of plastic. Lately,
I've craved frost
creeping like kudzu
because the pink heat
of summer has left me
in a state of decay.
After the cattails
collapse into themselves,
after the crawdads
retreat into the mud,
after the copperheads stop
sunning in the middle
of the road, after
the sun's chandelier crashes
low, there's only the rapture
of nature's preening
dormancy. Some distances,
say the length of a city
boardwalk or a dozen steps
between pine trees, create
an invisibility
that's impossible
to conquer, no matter
how high that vantage
floats. Forgive me

my emoting, diverging, the kick
of confessing—
I have but one dollar
and am loath to divide.

ANIMAL SCIENCE

Some type of squash or melon
        is growing from a mound
    of chicken shit in the backyard,

        so I imagine the seed passing
    through bowels, the chicken's skin
        waiting to be feathered
and the muscle waiting

to be deep-fried and consumed.
        Yesterday, I watched a woman scream
    at the man carrying their infant around

        the produce section at Walmart,
watched her hurl baby food
        and then cry by the grapes. The infant
stayed silent. Later, the same couple

strolled the bedding aisle,
        the man slipping his hand
down the back of her shorts.

        Near the end of their marriage,
    my parents bought a half-dozen
        box-store chickens.
We realized we had five roosters

and one hen months later. The roosters
        took turns mounting the hen, so we called
    her the slutty chicken and laughed

        until her back bled, raw and featherless.
One night she broke down the coop door,
        and we found her bowels strewn
about the yard by the neighbor's dog.

On a gravel road outside of town, a deputy
                is pulling over a young girl he's pulled over
    before because he knows about her

           fentanyl and when he finds it he asks
      Do you want to go to jail, or go home tonight?
              and unbuckles his duty belt. I know
    of no other animal that keeps poisoning

itself, Sodium Nitrate and Yellow #5,
                cheeseburgers and bourbon, the constant
    stream of shootings in the news

           reminding me I'm alive. I know
  my genes scream for continuity
           because my only purpose
  is to leave something useful. I used

to live near a landfill
                and would drive past to look at the trash
    being emptied

           from the garbage trucks, learning
  how filled the world is. Thinking about it now,
        I know I never saw a single
  blossom there.

IN THE WOODS

I could describe the minutiae
of moss,

                    the way leaves push

in summer,
        a birch sapling cowering
beneath a parent,

a fox
        in a hollowed-out tree,
            light shining
through foliage.

But none of that matters.

Just north of me: a tower's
        blinking strobe.

        I take a picture
           of a caterpillar,
because I know someone

who would like that. I smell the fresh

        clear-cut before I see it,
and I'm not appalled.

I just look
        down into my hands
           to find where I am.

THE ANATOMY OF ENVY

No silence at night in summer, just constant
katydid chatter flattering the trees. I envy
their translucence, the unforced music insect lives
bring, the way they know their immutable role
from birth. I envy them because I tire of watering
the garden by midsummer and let the plants return

to the dry dirt before the squash bugs return
and bury their future in the cracked fruit, constants
like gravity's claim on breath or the way water
fades and returns and fades enviably.
I've learned it's impossible to escape the rolling
drone of highway chatter, all their driving lives

droning like summer trees. I've learned life
is just a series of noises, leaving and returning
and moving on, offering nothing but a simple role
and a feeling of entrapment that grows constantly,
but never mind, entrapment is just sweltering envy—
envy like watching northern lights or a waterfall

through a screen, envy like watching a water
main erupt and living in drought, envy like living
with a child who only speaks to ghosts who envy
the living. All I want is a chance to return
and restart in the past because the constant
pathway of presence confuses my role.

I know of no one who understands their role.
If I were water, I'd understand myself, because water
lives with purpose, exists as a constant
whether violent or frozen or offering life.
If I were a singing tree, teeming and returning
every year, I'd be constant, enviable.

If I were a katydid I would have no envy,
wouldn't wince at understanding my role.
I would live simply like math, return
and be reborn each spring when water
thaws and offers opulence. I could live
without memory's bothersome constants

and envy, simple as a tree buzzing constantly
in summer, its innumerable insect lives
that know their return is as constant as water.

CONSIDERING ENTROPY

This was never about hummingbirds
        drifting too long into autumn—a chartreuse
or yellow-bellied charm faced skyward

on the sidewalk. Children might dare
        one another to pluck feathers to keep
in their pockets, their dirty fingers

staining the delicate keratin. This
        is about a gully's sustained change
after hard rain and how a kindergartener

might know how to stack prisms of blocks
        after one lesson, even though they're no
genius, never going to occupy

themselves with cancer cures or interstellar travel,
        instead staring cruelly down into a perfect
bird-feathered pocket. This is about the sea

forgetting two drops of rain falling
        in a clear sky, and a hummingbird, hovering
fast, fecund until entropy gives its ultimatum.

IN THE ATRIUM OF THE CHILDREN'S HOSPITAL

My son watches a model train
from a playground with fake grass.
Security guards x-ray entering bodies
and check bags. A riotous child
in a wheelchair spools past
as we wait, and I watch concern
grow on my son's face. I expect
him to ask questions, but he doesn't
as a too-thin preteen traces by.
I think I'm a narcissist because, standing
with all these parents and children
who'd rather take a dagger than be here,
I know that hunger has never
snatched my thoughts away,
that I've never been knocked out by gas,
had a growth cut from my body,
or been served sustenance
through a feeding tube. Knowing this,
and knowing my son is here
for a laparoscopic procedure, that he won't
stay for weeks or months like too many,
that my wife and I won't rent an apartment
next to the hospital and sell our house
because this place is hours from home,
makes me no anchor. Still,
as we pass from the atrium
into the bright sterility of the hospital,
my son takes my hand.

MODERN MEDICINE

Raspberries lose their gumption in late July.
They placate themselves, accept
becoming birdfeed to be dispersed

among conifers, to flow wordlessly
into the quagmire and wait for the snout
of next year. Their branches: mercury

in a newborn's fever. Their leaves
are like a spirometer testing an old woman's
lungs. Their roots: a lance through an abscess.

ARCHITECTURE

Like faith, a nail
    holds architecture
    dumbly together,

    careful as a toddler
touching a stove,
numb as a needle

in a tired vein.
    I've fallen from faith,
    moved slowly

    like waiting seconds,
exhausted from
the reckoning

of staring at the space
    I occupy. I've run
    from day to day, frayed

    like poverty's coats
and sofas, carts filled
with nothing

but what can be carried.
    All I see is rain, sunshine,
    clouds, clarity—all singing

    ballads that end
with a single
beaten drum.

ASK THE WIND TO BLOW

Full disclosure: I played bass
      in a worship band for three months
          and never felt moved, though

I wanted to. I wanted to weep
on an altar and look at the sky

      and feel. I wanted to bask, smile,
          be certain of certainty.

My dad tells this story
      of taking a Cessna into the woods
          to go hunting: the pilot looked

back at the three men and asked
their weight, then said *we'll give it a shot.*

      Now, I FaceTime my cancer-ridden mother,
          who keeps avoiding chemo

because she doesn't want
      to lose her blond hair.
          I tell her she should do it,

and she cries and feels something
while my toddler son touches her face

      through the smartphone
          screen. It's nearly spring, the church sign

says *Try God,* and I'm unsure
      just how to oblige.

THE FOG OF IT

Faith and molecules, the recurrence
    of biology, make a thick fog
        because sports fans believe in miracles.

I'm thankful for the sacrifices
    early humans made, to determine
what could be eaten and what was fatal,

the herbs best suited to season food.
      Most Anglo-Saxon words can be traced
        back to medical maladies, sickness

warrants elucidation where praise
    warrants looking again and again
until a flaw is found. Consider this:

one in ten thousand acorns become oaks,
    but cowbirds lay their eggs
        in songbird nests, make homes

in what another built.
    The worst song in the world, the worst,
isn't "We Built This City" or any song

by Justin Bieber. Rather, it's a two-chord chant
    written by a half-savant child and sung
        to his mother while she sat on her bed and wept.

FOR CERTAIN

—For my friend B.R., murdered by his wife and her lover while taking out the trash.

I failed math in middle school,
      because he showed me how Mentos
could be spit through a straw

      at the teacher—how algebra
was really an excuse to carve lyrics
      into a desk.

+

Someone I was certain
I would never leave gifted
me a slip joint
knife, but every time
I opened it my hand bled,
and we split like skin
on an operating table.

+

This isn't my story to tell,
      but it was skip day

in high school
      and everyone was high—

a teen girl told a teen boy
      she would fuck him if he swam
      across the river and back.

The cold crept into his quadriceps.
Their stoned smiles were swept away.
The divers snatched at the bottom.

\+

The last time I spoke to him, we were ordering
                Chinese for our families near the town
we grew up in. We talked about playing music

        ten years ago, his rapping snare, double kick
drums, my Telecaster plugged into a now-sold
        half-stack, both of us trying and failing to stay in time.

\+

If my wife
                were to murder me,
    I think it'd be with poison.

    Maybe. I don't know.

Cyanide in the soup
                a few nights in a row.

\+

He didn't know. He fought with his wife
    about money or children the night before
and maybe pictured a lover sealing her mouth

    with his mouth. He bagged his trash and headed
to the curb and knew, soon, he would sit at the table
    and have dinner with his son and daughter.

WISH LIST WHILE READING THE NEWS ON MY PHONE

Give me celebs failing so I can watch
    their loves and lives devolve to spectacles
for Google to decipher and distribute, pitch
    to proper demographics. I'm skeptical,

but let the weather radar be accurate
    because the ground is filling with dark cracks
and dust. Show me the baseball score, no, get
    highlight reels on repeat, so I can keep track

of what truly matters. Find me stupid
    videos so I laugh, because the news
is someone killing another, muted
    lives authorities save for later use.

Let this ad for a better night of sleep
    be true, give me something useful to keep.

HALF-STAFF

Which influencer
    died and created

    this malaise,
which city endured

a gunman?
    The flags look

    dead as the crowns
of two oaks

that spent years
    choking one another,

    braided
together like rope.

DEPARTING IN A SPACE SHUTTLE

Maybe the first story
about magic,   a protagonist's
triumph,   love love love
is really a snare.

                         The first book
I remember: shape-shifters
and aliens slinking
into the brain to control
the body like a shooter game—

                     now three men huddle
around a smartphone
to watch a bikini model
dance to "Teenage Dream."

    A replay,   their mouths open
as it goes slow motion
      and they wonder how to get wives
or girlfriends to wear lace,
        to romp on the bar barefoot.
                I can watch every pitch
of a baseball game,

                            subtle
cutter break,   a foul
into the dugout or seats
scattering fans who stand
in replica jerseys, applaud
the spectacle of crowds
and rounding third.

          Maybe
it was nostalgia,
    but my grandmother
said she never felt

so close to her father
as when Orson Welles
broadcast an invasion
over the radio.

                                                She hid
in his arms and imagined
Nazi tanks and stomping troops,
    or a death ray,
        how things would end.

EXHIBIT A

On screen tackle + zero percent financing
    for well-qualified buyers + sleep aid

restless leg antacid ads + dollar fifty burger + storms
    along the coast + ribbons of paper smiles

        LED smiles + Have you seen
what lies beyond the swirling galaxy and infinitude?

    Have you seen
scenes? Buy a larger screen to see

clarity. Buy a larger screen to see exactness
    + to see nature natural

      A certain fracture
of the populace believes

+ Elvis Lives + Have you tasted the shape
    of a mouth + outline of shoulders

      + filled stadiums + headlit highways
    + weather report disparity

news disparity + updates in bold text
    for emphasis

distinct as floodwater + loud like a quarry
      conveyor + so many plummeting stones

LEGACY WASTE

Ever since my cousin
joined the Special Forces,
    all he talks about is training—
                      being drowned,
  resuscitated,   drowned,
dropped off in the sea to tread water.

    The military is not involved with X
but *I have seen* X.

    On the way to work,   I drive past
a closed school: frames of swing sets
behind chain links,   boarded windows
  the walls lined with asbestos.

    A few miles away,
a landfill smolders a hundred feet
below the surface.

                    The heat
keeps spreading closer
to nuclear waste a munition factory
buried fifty years ago.

                On the news,
  specialists say it is safe,
  even if the fire reaches
it poses no threat
to anyone's health.

    There was a rash
of Hodgkin's disease
at my high school—
                maybe
the children played too close

to the railroad tracks,
>	maybe something seeped
into the aquifer,	into kitchen sinks.

>	Back then,	I dated a girl in remission.

>	We sat in my car listening
to *Bat Out of Hell*.
I started to kiss
her neck.
>	My hands
recoiled when they brushed
>	the port in her chest.

TATTOO REMOVAL

Outside, there's a patrolman searching a Toyota Camry
with a Gadsden flag bumper sticker.
The driver, handcuffed, stares down at the curb.

I, too, keep a loaded pistol in my nightstand
because I'm tired of hearing about robberies
and all the dead children in the Middle East,

their blanketed bodies laid down in rows
to be identified or unidentified, their tongues
tranquil and silenced. Some nights, I unload

the magazine, and the brass rounds slip out
to roll along the floor. I watch as the cop pushes
the driver's head down, guiding him in and away.

CROWDSOURCING

I am not the woman who waters every quick-dying
flower in the children's graveyard, wipes pollen
from splinters of headstones. I am not the hairy man—
hip-length alpaca mane—who stands on the side
of the intersection with a guitar slung across his belly,
both middle fingers pointed at passerby but smiling.
I am not ice without kerosene, nor Vaseline without
the lounge of flesh. I am not a fox, in any sense, nor
the beard of a turkey being chased across the forest floor.
I am not the natural cacophony of ambient sound
a forest makes, nor anger erupting from a father
who peaked in high school. I am not dreams lost
in the labor of barns and fields, dreams lost to air
turbulence and experiment. I am not a poison pump,
though a final squelch of breath might tell you otherwise.

DOCTOR, DOCTOR

Fix my kinked spine

                with a phalanx
of titanium vertebrae. Transform

my crown into a lighthouse,

        and buttress my femurs with figured
mahogany—seal them tight.

Flake this apple's skin—

        no, judder it off
with a slick machine, zip it away

into sycophantic usefulness.

        Pestle my gnarled
core into pectin.

    See here—

        uniformity
like old cells dividing.

CHILD DRAWINGS

I think it's a moon—no—it's an ocean
    of people singing,
    though the water

    is Salmon, and their skins
are Bluetiful. In the Razzmatazz
grass, the wax like petrichor—

a wingless bird,
    an accidental cicada dangling
    from the predator's beak.

    Imagine this: the ethereal
white space between wavering
Cornflower line and half-filled highlight,

an accidental cast shadow,
    the broken, Spring Green wings
    of a butterfly, the crooked face

    slope shape a child sees—
the world as sequences
of Periwinkle geometry.

STARS AND SATELLITES

When I look at the night
    sky, I know it's insignificant whether
I can identify the star or satellite
    preparing the same advertisement

playlist for all my digital devices.
    It's insignificant because a certain
fracture of the populace believes
    most birds are drones, so at the last

family gathering an aunt and uncle
    explained how to distinguish God's
creature from government oversight
    by watching: the drones have rigid wings

and birds fly naturally. Last time
    I registered a vehicle with a credit
bureau, they knew where I frequently park,
    who I ride with, what my friends drive,

all the options of who I am
    laid out in neat little rows
on the screen for me to select.
    Yesterday afternoon, a vulture flew

overhead, its wings unmoving
    in the windless air. I watched it circle
through binoculars until the bird blinked,
    flapped and landed on whatever

death it chose to eat. I keep reading
    about another management team failing
their subordinates, this time
    a collapsed building and sifting rubble,

the discoveries unmentionable.
    It's insignificant, unmentionable,
but last night, I swore a satellite
    crept closer as I took out the trash.

PERFIDY

I like to feed
my three-year-old lemons
to watch his lips
pucker like a cancer
mole. I feel worthless
when I stare at verdant
tree lines, because the tacky
insides of fresh-cut trees
preen like crows beaking
what I assumed
was their clavicles,
until Google brought
forth *furcula*.
My algorithm
is now distorted
by exploded views
of avian frames,
advertisements
for birding lessons,
lessons on discerning
an oaks age by cutting
it open like sour citrus.
Another way to waste
time is to measure
heaps of gravel piling
out of a truck bed,
waiting for it
to scatter. Still another—
watch myodesopsia
flower like supernovas,
bright and brief as birth.
No amount of soap
can wash away
time's marauding thistles.
I've never located
a whale, never footed

another continent,
meaning I'm squandered
like an iron machine
in the salt and rain.

CUTTING WOOD

                   No tenderness
swings a maul, no cherry stump

fruits once decay seeps deep.

I had a sense of humor once. Say
a squashed spider exhaled a name,

stated it right there on the floor

as its juices leaked into the rug—
I used to know a joke about that,

but now it's wasted away by time's boundless

                  amble. As the maul
gnaws through lumber,

I'm left with little but prayers

and a stump, a simple place
                  to sit and watch the sun.

WISH LIST FOR A DEITY

Hide my guilt in the robes of infinity.
    Forgive my vices and replace my thoughts
with an iPhone—I don't want to compute
    how many scratcher tickets I need buy

to pay what is owed. Cure my soft body
    of orange soda, mechanically
separated meat parts. Forgive me
    for shooting a mostly road-killed raccoon—

too precious to stay half-dead in the road—
    in the face. Grant me favor and fervor,
silver thrones guaranteed in the cosmos
    because nothing's terror always drives me,

nothing's terror is all that's left once guilt
    is reckoned. Please tell me which way to live.

WHISKEY GOSPEL

I spent childhood
captive in a bar—
weeknight billiard
lessons with a man
who shot dimes
off his Chevy
for bets to make rent.
He lined up trick shots
while my parents
drunk danced
to the endless jukebox.
The tavern
employed one bartender
who paid herself well
in well whiskey
and would, before closing,
have enough
to proclaim herself
the messiah, though
her gospel never traveled
because she feared
the interstate. I never
finessed a massé shot,
never became indoctrinated,
but learned some old men
judged the corn
in their gardens
by how fat
the earworms grew
before harvest,
how some old men
wanted to vodka fight
everyone before they died
yellow of liver cancer—
clenched fists, final words.

THE GREAT RACCOON WAR

    Slipping beneath tin sheets
of pole barns, devouring
        cattle feed and corn.   *Shoot them on sight.*

    They only come at night.   *Set out poison.*
A mother and kit skid
        down trees, tiny thumbs thumbing

    noses. A dozen furred bodies
in a shed one night, poisoned
        tongues forever licking gravel.   *Poison is better than lead, get the*
                                                       dead ones out of the shed.

    One hisses from a trap, smiles
before slipping
        into the drowning bucket.

    Another gives birth in a crawl space.   *Beneath the floor. They're beneath us*
Chattering like wind chimes in a storm.   *Set out poison shoot them on sight.*
        One night a snarler snaggled

    with the dog. Another night
the trash emptied on the lawn.   *They are unafraid.*
        Another one swelling.

    Another curdles   *They have grown bold.*
the night air. Another thought killed
        returns and ambulates.

DROGUE

I spend too much time
thinking about how many lungs
seized and stopped
before someone learned
pokeweed was poisonous,
or about who discovered
whale blubber could be boiled
and chopped down into oil
to illuminate the dark
or scrub a body.
What I mean—I'm not
a scientist, won't find
a magnificent new breed
of bird deep in the forest.
I won't find a way
to build a tuba without
brass, nor find a use
for pocket lint. Last night,
I found two dead maggots
in a bottle of bourbon and learned
I don't speak with a guttural roar,
instead my voice is a silent,
wide-open mouth.

THE ANATOMY OF THE COLD

I knelt, gutting trout, by creek water
while my son practiced skipping stones.
Too cold to stay, we left without a word
and strode like crows through snow into a field
until the low sun hoisted once-roosted lives
into the southern sky, some staying to cross

presence with absence, like a crossed-
out line in a sermon. The air was still like water
at the top of a puddle before a foot brings life
to the flat silence. I carry a breath of stones
with me and the weight becomes a field
of crops covered in early snow because words

are meaningless to nature. How many words
would a coyote need to kill a rabbit, to cross
into suburbia and invade everything from open fields
to dumpsters stuffed with chain food and foul water?
How many sons and fathers walk past the same stone
before it turns to dirt? How many pass the same cold life

of learning how to pretend to be alive,
trading all their minutes for the right words?
When it's cold, breathing is like throwing stones
toward a scarecrow preening on a cross
who still asks the wind for fresh water
and somewhere warm to sleep instead of the field.

When it's cold, it's easy to picture a frozen field
to lie down in until spring, when flesh grows life
and the news tells another story. Sometimes, when water
freezes, it expands and cracks everything like words
from a distant memory, leaving something like a cross
between childhood and the etching in a gravestone

decaying over decades. After hands become stones
in the cold, there's nothing left except a field
of histories someone begs an idol fixed to a cross
to forgive. I know nothing of that—I've lived
through forgiveness too many times to remember the words.
I know how much forgiveness is like a pool of water,

ordinary and impermanent until the impact from a stone.
I know the same water is like a father and son crossing
a field, where life learns to speak its first words.

TRASH PILE

The neighbors always burn
their trash: acrid smoke wafts
    through the open window—
    diapers and tires,
plastic and Styrofoam, aluminum.
        Their streetlight
shadows dance across
    the rebel battle flag
painted on the side of their shed.

    I rode the bus during middle school,
and there was a little boy
who always sat next to his older brother.
    One spring, the older brother boarded
alone once, twice,   a month.
We all asked, though everyone knew,
a town of 678 always knows, what happened

    The boy said *Dad will be home soon,*
or *I will be out of the hospital*
next week
    and when he finally returned,
his face was scarred as war metal.

    They burned their trash
in a barrel, and the older brother
wanted to see an aerosol can
explode.
    Now, when something detonates
at the neighbors', I smell
burnt flesh, chlorofluorocarbon,
think of the boy's lipless smile.

BULL RIDERS

I'm not sure why my wife and I did it, but the sign
said *Bull Ride Ahead,* and we obliged

because we needed to be satiated
and spectacles are everything.
                                        Now, a bullfighter

pours kerosene in the dirt and lights it on fire
for the riders to walk through as they're introduced,

each of them as desperate as the fractured face
of a cowboy I bought a horse from years ago.

They pull the gate and a flash
of muscled hide kicks and bucks the rider,

bright chaps blossoming the night sky.
They pull the gate, muscled hide flashes

against the crowd, and I think of transience.
They pull the gate and a flash of muscled hide

kicks and the rider stays hitched until the buzzer,
leaps off, stumbles, and receives a retaliatory stomp

in the abdomen. The crowd gasps, but the rider stands
and tips his straw hat, walks bow-legged

to the gate, imagining morning,
the green and yellow of the bruise.

GRIM SANITY

I didn't see the gravity
      of the dilemma, the grim
      sanity of it, until later
as I listened to my three-year-old
      scold the sin his mother

and I committed by letting
      his infant brother cry for a few
dim moments—*he needs food!*
      he declared while our infant
      wailed. I thought of a story

I'd heard, or read, or been witness
      to and the way some memories
      resurface like cancer or bad habits:
a young mother, seduced by a swain
      of opiates, shot a whole gram

of Carfentanyl into her vein,
      the dam of her body breaking
loose until she went down dead
      on the floor. Her two children
      stayed alone for days. They found

the infant cold, still, scrambled
      eggs covering his mouth, neck,
      shoulders. The older brother
just ran away from anyone
      who tried to hold him.

GUNSHOT AT THE NEIGHBORS'

Muffled by a pillow
or it could have been
something heavy falling.
Never mind, the walls
are thick but I still hear
them fight then fuck
because I guess that's how
some couples are.
I remember sighting
in rifles into a pasture
when I was young
the neighbors peering
out their windows.
When I drive at night
I think of how every headlight
on a two-lane road
is a deathtrap, blown tire
or text message,
a ravine full of trees.

THE DEEP BLUE OF NEPTUNE

        Line up a pelican, a crane,
and a stork and I won't

be able to tell the difference,
nor abalone from mother-

        of-pearl, a copperhead from a bull snake—
berate me or I'll do it myself.

A hawk is a hawk,
glass is translucent,
                and photos
used to require impossible stillness.

    +

There's no cure
for seeing a crash like this—
the hood and quarter panels
crushed back into the firewall,
the cabin unspeakable.
                I had
a friend once who worked
for a wrecker company,
and he could barely speak
for weeks after towing a van
where a man had shot himself
in the driver's seat.

All he would say
was he was the low man
on the crew, then mumble
about cups of bone and brain.

    +

What I crave—fresh paint

over a rusted car roof,
aidless sleep, a stuffed

        gutter to run my naked fingers
through: dead leaves and twigs

turn to dirt if left alone
to fend for themselves.

    +

I remember a neighbor

who had a crop duster plane
in his shed: he never flew,

but would get whiskey drunk
and cotton mouthed, sit red-faced

and stern in the tattered cockpit,
his family mixing milk

        and water, calling it dinner.

DETOURS

I drive past an old stone Catholic church. The stained glass
shines and the steeple looms, limestone, towering
over everything in the town of one-fifty.
When there's time, I pull into the parking lot to stare
at the oak doors and think about what sort
of battering ram I would need
                              to get in,
how that type of oak can survive
a house fire that melts appliances and cast iron.
The church sign quotes the passage in the bible
that reads *You should be as quick to pray*
as you are to text,
and I think of being selfish.
                         The last time
I took my son to the pediatrician, the nurse
wore a crucifix outside her scrubs. When she took
his temperature, I saw them: three streaking scars
running parallel to her radius and ulna, and I could
only think of what music she must've listened to when
the blade slipped into her skin, whether
she had been found
                              or saved. I know nothing of deliverance
but was in a boat once when I saw a man praying.
He looked skyward, made the sign of the cross,
then stepped over the side and slipped beneath.

BROKEN PANTOUM UPON GETTING A NEW PHONE NUMBER

Whoever had this number before me
must have great credit. I get text messages
and robo voicemails offering loans
double my salary and I hover over the link

offering credit. I get text messages
from a car dealer or megachurch and imagine
doubling my salary and discovering the link
between cars, god, and making enough money

to interest a car dealer or megachurch. I imagine
acceptance, how survival is a simple roulette
of god, cars, and making enough money
to be content.   If I had great credit

I'd be accepted, survive the roulette
and cut ties, head to the Yukon
and be content living on great credit,
thriving on solar panels and latrines.

If I cut ties and head to the Yukon,
I could be erased,
                no more Googling my name
because I'd thrive on solar panels and latrines.
        Then I think of whoever had this number dying

how they were erased, no more Googling their name.
The family, left with nothing but a voicemail greeting

from whoever had this number and died
might cling to a name
                being spoke clear and slow.

They were left with nothing but a voicemail greeting
and fights over money and inheritance,
>							how to stop

clinging to a name being spoke clear and slow
I know in a few weeks,
>							the calls will end

and I won't think of fights over money and inheritance
or a family trying to pray
>							the dead out of purgatory.

I know in a few weeks, the calls will end,
whoever's memory
>							will fade into mirage

or a family trying to pray them out of purgatory
and convince themselves
>							some memories aren't real,

how those memories fade into faithful mirage.
Every time I start to think of faith or god,
>							I start

to convince myself some memories   aren't real,
how god is like a robo voicemail
>							offering loans and credit.

Every time I think of talking to god,   I start wondering

>   who had this number before me.

SHUDDER

Easy enough to ignore
    on the horizon line,
are the blinking strobes

beaming down
    data so omniscience

    can be pulled from pockets,

or are they unexplained aerial
    phenomena loitering
just above the atmosphere?

Jets take off like gunshots
    around here, making it easy

    to imagine a fighter

giving chase to a discoid
    spaceship, Google
alien sightings, evidence.

I've made a habit
    of lying about memories,

    but as a child,

truly, I looked out a window,
    and saw a swirling circle
of brilliant, unnatural

light, then it fluttered
    and was gone.

    Now every morning

I flinch after loud noises,
      a missed call
or unanswered text, assume

ruin because of routines,
      imagine a bomb

dropping two states away

while families eat
      breakfast grits and oranges,
their Styrofoam plates boiling.

DEAD SWEETHEART

*—for someone whose name faded, 1994-20something, Painted Rock
Conservation Area, Westphalia, MO*

Every tribute I read—this one's
    a Disney quote—leads to imagining
a face: low cheekbones and dark hair,
    dark eyes, maybe a snaggled canine
because orthodontists are expensive,
    and their parents were poor.

This hand-painted memorial
    says it was written by someone young
who loved pastel colors. Overlooking
    the Osage River from a high bluff,
where natives are said to have buried
    their dead, I keep reading

the Disney quote, moving
    in all its sentiment. I then think
of blood entering a syringe, an exhale
    and a bright pulse then fading, a friend
finding a friend on a couch after a party
    in the pale first stage

of rigor mortis, or a ruptured aneurysm
    or leukemia creeping through the body
like a vine, or a rope across
    a larynx, becoming silenced,
becoming simple words
    left on a stone by a river.

WISH LIST WHILE LISTENING TO LOVE SONGS

Unfold my love like this: eyes, body parts,
pheromones taking control, then laments
for mortgages, children, learning the art
of time's claim, what forever must've meant.

Tell me what I need say to make her stay
despite my endless faults. Don't let our song
be a murder ballad. Cue the deep bass
thump so we can try to dance now, but wrong,

our feet out of time like a solar clock
in a century of dark, wrong like rain
sliding up windows, or a spit of rock
that expands instead of erodes. No shame

in wondering what it means to stay young
and loving, what words will be left unsung.

WHILE DRIVING

Remember: think only of childhood
after eating hallucinogens. Anticipate
chemical responses when mixing solvents.
Don't tell the patrolman there's a gun
in the trunk and act thankful
for the speeding ticket. Change the oil:
5w20 for winter and summer and anytime.
Translate this to blessings, amen. Remember
mom and dad going to a Methodist church
before they divorced, the old women
reaching out their hands. Avoid blessings—
they are usually selfish. Avoid stubbing toes
on religious texts or living room walls.
Remember the time the grill caught fire
and dad put water on it and the fire
got worse so the vinyl siding melted
and we ordered pizza. Always be thankful
for cheeseburgers. Look in the rearview mirror
to make sure nothing is leaking.
Get the tires rotated. Drive away
but mind what follows.

NIGHT SONG

This moment,
in the evening's

bare dark—
a shudder

of wing, owl
gliding, warm

and silent
in the bare

sky. I ignore
the present—

no trace
of the ground's

infinitudes, people
who speak once

then disappear
as a large crowd,

the labor
of one another.

The moon wakes,
unmasked, away

from the parallel
the crowd failed

to draw—forgotten.
Darkness forces

itself into the bare
sky. There,

though something
remains unsaid,

there is something
staying still out-

side of me—the lack
of sky and cells,

light,
darkness.

CIGARETTE VENDING MACHINE

Say an emphysema patient lights
    a Pall Mall at the bar,
       sallow and thin skin, swallowing
down the stagnant air. An advertisement
dances across the screen—a self-correcting
Mitsubishi, better mileage, no loss of power.

I can't stop thinking of the stainless shine
of restaurant tables, livened walls levying
life and satiated hunger—
                      those bleeding ulcers,
the meat ground so fine.

    They took out the cigarette vending
machine yesterday, time- and smoke-eroded
Marlboro logo, the levers grasping
    the ground as trashmen dragged
       it to the door. The next commercial
is for a stop-smoking aid, but he pays
no attention,

                    just tugs on the brown filter
while thinking of carburetor cleaner
and chrome, the steel hood of an AMC
Rambler, the nostalgia of vinyl seats,
a steering wheel so thin it can cut a man in half.

ENTROPY'S ULTIMATUM

Not fire,
>   but the overlooked

>   splicing of calamity
>   and belief. Not

>   coy dares—
instead a series

>   of braying prayers
>   for permanence—

the way fleas
>   declare themselves,

>   not with a glare,
>   but with their wordless

>   mouthparts. Not
an ambulance's

>   blaring siren
>   seizing silence

or a galactic all-mother,
>   but torches

>   warily wavering,
>   their flicker fade

>   blaze like a limbless
tree, present

>   but empty. Not
>   the allure

the unseen offers,
> like distant music

>> or the smell
>> of burning hickory,

>> but the way
> bacteria burgeons,

>>> the buoyance
>>> of presence.

PEST CONTROL

The first hard frost brings silence
and mercy to the trees—
                      but mice creep

      into pantries, chew loaves of bread, cereal,

   pip in the walls like children at play.

I set out snap traps because glue
ends in a sticky scrap
                    and d-CON brings

     in more, a sweet treat before bedtime.

   The bastards lick the peanut butter

clean off the trap's catch, thumbs on their noses
like a quick boxer
                    dipping a cross.

       Nothing is enviable about mice—except

    their proliferate breeding, naked pink

babies nesting in trash. Once, as a child,
my dad found a hole
                    in our baseboard

     because mice had been chewing

   through our food, tiny gluttons—

he filled a Shop-Vac quarter-full of water
and stuck the hose
                  into the mouse hole:

    their little bodies made a thud against the hard

  plastic of the bucket, their tiny feet

cycling until exhaustedly
drowning in their own
      wet vacuumed nest.

     My brother and I: small but cognizant,

  took to smashing the strays

with unopened moving boxes, or shooting
them with pellet guns, their lead-riddled

      bodies writhing until laying

  still as frost's mercy.

EXHIBIT B

Car crash traffic   (slow and steady spectators)
+ news shooting + millions of views

because a cacophony of flashing cameras
always draws notice + shirtless

influencer   (influencing) + too inundated
(with light) to care about thoughts anymore

+ Google morphing
the world's history

      into a pocket + YouTube TikTok
tutorials   (car maintenance)   (weight lift)

(watching a product unboxed)
+ presence presents present by reaching

through a screen to touch
a face +   (a museum of plastic bodies)

(a museum of wax bodies)
a museum of bodies with their hands

      outstretched   (smiling selfie)
+ living as an empty theme park

      (how the pixels fade)
          (how the pixels sharpen)

WISH LIST AFTER USING A 3-D PRINTER

Please print our slices of pizza
        so we don't have to go outside
or greet the driver.
                Print a mask to hide

our faces from ourselves
        and one another. Print
a Glock .40 in case someone
                comes through the open window.

Print a tangible god
        to provide an escape
from the constant terror
                of becoming nothing.

Print a bronze statue
        to topple at a protest/riot,

the noun to chosen
        by the news network

we believe most. Print us
        a pint of bourbon
because every Monday
        we say goodbye

and hello and goodbye.
        Print us a new
friend   or spouse   or child
        because we are surprised

to feel alone in a place
        so filled. Print now a new shield
because if we're gunpowder,
        that makes god raw brass.

TRAFFIC

Google my name
    and a mustached man
      wearing a Stetson hat
appears alongside a fifty-state
map of my name.

I've never
    been to Oklahoma
    but it's shaded red
because more of me lives
      there than anywhere else

    +

When I turn
    on a light switch
something shocks

    me—maybe the wires
are faulty
    or I've become as static

as an auto-filled
    term populating
a search bar.

    +

The constant shock
    of news
    is like a cilice
reminding me I'm as flawed
      as tomorrow,

as imperfect as a creek bed
    after a week of rain,

      an algorithm
brought to life
          by sequences

and arithmetic,
          a target demographic.

    +

No snow
last Christmas day.

My family exchanged
      department store/Amazon
      gifts and drank wine
so we could speak.

When I left
there was no traffic.

THE ANATOMY OF FORGIVENESS

I give nothing to nature, so I've bought bees
to keep in my backyard—their tiny lives
offer meaning to mine, will clear the air
of the errors I've made since being born.
Thinking of nature reminds me to forgive
faults, because bees are faultless, and to sow

seed in the ground: squash and melons, peppers, so
all summer I can eat fruit and bloom while the bees
harvest, build, clean, feed, and die, forgiving
through sacrifice. I've spent too much time simply living
through cold and disease, fixating on being reborn
and forgiven, breathing a flood of clean air.

I've spent too much time deciding how much air
I wasted last year, how much life needs resewing
to correct the wreck brought forth by being born
to consume. I know nothing, but the bees
are an escape because keeping something small alive
is simple. They're like faith taking hold to forgive

living like a storm, an existence as forgiving
as floodwater. I know nothing, but breaths of air
are another escape, the automatic constant of living
taking a toll from the dirt I live in, the dirt I sow
and mold to suit my want. I've never thought to be
anything but a cold life, continually reborn

as a disease—I live like an airborne
plague infecting the ground around me, forgiving
forests with a series of machines. I want to be
like rain, vital to tough ground and calm air,
offer more than just the constant sowing
of calamity, more than the endless parade of living

with excess massing around me. I want to keep alive
something small, something which had been born
with a purpose other than to consume so
I can atone for my existence, offer forgiveness
rather than continue living as wasted air
while I devour my surroundings. Let's just say the bees

will sow a series of waxing sinew, offer life
back into being, as they are born and reborn
in the forgiveness of the bright spring air.

ACKNOWLEDGMENTS

I would like to send endless gratefulness and love to my wife Christine, my sons Barrett and Wilder, and the rest of my family for giving me the time and support to complete the poems in this collection.

I am incredibly honored by Alison Hawthorne Deming for selecting this collection as the winner of the 2024 Stan and Tom Wick Poetry Prize. Thank you to all involved in the selection process.

Without my friend and mentor Sara Burge's weekly accountability, this project would have never been completed, so I am immensely appreciative for her ideas and support. I'd also like to express sincere thanks and offer respect for the faculty and peers I worked with at the University of Nebraska-Omaha and Missouri State University, whose tutelage and feedback helped shape my ideas and helped me develop and refine the work in this collection. I'd also like to thank Soon Jones, Jamie Wendt, Cid Galicia, Molly O'Dell, Kiara Nicole Letcher, and Shyla Shehan for their ideas and feedback in our workshop.

Grateful acknowledgment is made to the following publications in which these poems, some of which appeared in earlier drafts, first appeared:

"Departing in a Space Shuttle"	*Beecher's Magazine*
"Tattoo Removal"	*Tar River Poetry*
"Wish List While Reading the News on My Phone"	*Tar River Poetry*
"Ask the Wind to Blow"	*Skink Beat Review*
"While Driving"	*Third Wednesday*
"In the Woods"	*Solar*
"Dead Sweetheart"	*American Journal of Poetry*
"Trash Pile"	*American Journal of Poetry*
"Gunshot at the Neighbors'"	*American Journal of Poetry*
"Legacy Waste"	*Meridian*
"Detours"	*Storm Cellar*
"Bull Riders"	*Book of Matches*
"Stars and Satellites"	*Split Rock Review*

"Cigarette Vending Machine"	*The Fourth River*
"Animal Science"	*West Trade Review*
"Wish List After Using a 3-D Printer"	*West Trade Review*
"Modern Medicine"	*Drunk Monkeys*
"The Anatomy of the Cold"	*Southern Humanities Review*
"The Anatomy of Forgiveness"	*North Meridian Review*
"Half-Staff"	*North Meridian Review*
"Shudder"	*North Meridian Review*
"For Certain"	*Jet Fuel Review*
"Considering Entropy"	*Flint Hills Review*
"Whiskey Gospel"	*Slab Literary Magazine*
"Broken Pantoum upon Getting a New Phone Number"	*Pinch*
"Traffic"	*Pacifica Literary Review*

"Ask the Wind to Blow" also won the 2022 Helen W. Kenefick Poetry Prize through the Academy of American poets and subsequently appears on the Academy of American Poets website.

"Wish List After Using a 3-D printer" also won the 2023 Helen W. Kenefick Poetry Prize through the Academy of American poets and subsequently appears on the Academy of American Poets website.